CREDIT REPAIR SECRETS

HOW TO FIX YOUR CREDIT AND REMOVE YOUR NEGATIVE ACCOUNTS FOREVER. 609 LETTER TEMPLATES FOR YOUR PERSONAL BALANCE

Table of Contents

Introduction 1

Chapter 1. Basics of Credit Repair 4

Chapter 2. Is Credit Repair Ethical? 10

Chapter 3. Self-Credit Repair Step........................ 22

Chapter 4. The Debt Snowball................................ 29

Chapter 5. What Is Section 609 33

Chapter 6. General Advice to See Success With 609 . 42

Chapter 7. How to Proceed with The Letters 51

Chapter 8. The Templates You Need (609 Letter) 59

Chapter 9. How to Boost Your Credit Score 100+ Points?.. 69

Chapter 10. How to Find Credit Cards with Guaranteed Approval?... 76

Chapter 11. What the Credit Bureaus and The Lawyers Do Not Want You to Know 82

Chapter 12. How Credit Scores Are Calculated 86

Chapter 13. Right Mindset for Credit Management 91

Chapter 14. Delete Inquiries on Your Report 97

Chapter 15. Rebuild Your Credit 105

Chapter 16. Protect Your Credit: Credit Monitoring . 111

Conclusion 117

Introduction

Most of us know that a poor credit score can prevent us from getting a loan or a credit card, but many of us don't know that it can also affect other areas of our lives such as: A poor credit score can prevent you from getting a job or a promotion. Employers are permitted by federal and many state laws to use your credit history in hiring decisions, believing that how someone handles their financial responsibilities is an indication of how well they might handle their work responsibilities as well.

The better your personal credit status is, the better chance you have of getting a start-up loan or a loan to expand your business. Most investors and lenders want to be confident in the financial status of the principals in the company, in particular their credit status. The theory being that if you cannot manage your own finances, how can you handle those of a business? Also, if you are selling a product and your credit status is good, the manufacturer of the product may be more likely to front you the product and allow you to pay for it after.

How much your credit status affects insurance is somewhat dependent on state laws. Your credit status may affect your rates or types of homeowner, rental, or car insurance. Some auto insurance companies believe that poor credit correlates to a higher accident risk and require higher premiums.

Buying a home is a big step and unless you can pay for it in cash, you will need a loan. This means everything involved comes down to your credit score and credit report. They will determine if you can even get a loan. If you can get a loan, they will determine the amount, type, and interest rate of the loan. It may also affect purchases you never thought about such as your homeowner's insurance, and necessities for the home such buying a refrigerator or a bed on credit.

More reasons, a poor credit score can keep you from renewing a professional license or prevent you from getting utilities or cable connections in your new apartment/home. It can also prevent you from posting bail for yourself or someone else. There are literally hundreds of ways a poor credit score can negatively impact your life, and what is more, it can do so for years to come, if you do not act on it.

In fact, poor credit can easily cost you thousands of dollars a year in higher interest, larger fees, bigger premiums, extra loan points, and other hidden costs.

Not only that, but a single negative item on your credit report will haunt you for years. On the other hand, having a high score will get you credit when and where you need it. It increases your chances for landing better jobs, getting lower interest rates and fees. This is not only convenient but can save you thousands of dollars over a period of time.

Now, let us understand the basics of credit repair.

Chapter 1. Basics of Credit Repair

It is hard to navigate today's society using credit. A variety of companies use your credit to choose also to place the pricing for services and goods that you use and also whether to do business. Consumers using a credit history seek out credit repair to increase their credit to have a simpler time.

What is Bad Credit?

Bad credit is when you have missed one or more payments throughout your life, be it your fault or not. The most common mistake people make is not defaulting on a payment, it is actually delaying payments. It is usually when you forget about a deadline or can't find a certain bill and you end up not paying, or being late, which in the eyes of the people borrowing money makes you look a bit financially unstable. Sometimes, even if you have had impeccable behavior, you are unfortunately affected by the loss of a job. Becoming unemployed has such grave consequences and lead to your assets being repossessed or even bankruptcy. Even if you went through a similar phase and you have bounced back, having this kind of history will impact your credit report in a negative way for a very long period of time.

It can also happen to you to be the victim of an error, even if you have not missed a single payment on your credit card until now. An error in the bank's system or an error from the parties responsible for building your credit report will affect you nonetheless, and so will fraud and abuse. Fraud cases are rare, but their consequences are costly. Fraud happens when someone uses your identity to submit a credit application, they get it and then they do not repay it anymore. You will be contacted by the bank and until you can prove you have been the target of a scam; you can have a tough time. Abuse generally refers to when you are oblivious with your expenses and spend over your credit card limit. You can wake up one day to a huge amount of debt and cases of abuse most often end in you being forced to declare bankruptcy. In order to avoid these cases, you need to be very careful with your finances, but regardless of what your situation is, usually there is a solution or a set of measures you can enforce to prevent it.

How to Avoid Bad Credit?

First of all, if you have lost your main source of income and are not able to make your payments in time or at all, it is important you say so. Announcing the fact that you may be unable to pay in the following months might land you a grace period from the lender. That means that you will not suffer any penalties for a given period of time, until you can get back on your feet, maybe get a new job and you can resume your normal payments.

You have to prioritize bills, meaning you will have to make a few judgements calls on what bills you should pay with the money you have left, and which ones might be less likely to affect your credit. Keeping up with your bills is difficult, but it is also important if you do not want to end up with bad credit. Use your savings or whatever else you have available and you may be able to make your credit look good even if you went through losing your job. These methods work to prevent credit, but they also apply in the case of you doing damage control. A credit repair will be a lot easier if you benefitted from a grace period and do not have as many past due bills. It shows you were concerned and aware of the situation and that you tried your best to remain in control of your finances.

What Is Credit Repair?

Credit repair is the process in which credit standing is fixed, which might have declined due to various reasons. Credit standing might be as straightforward as disputing the information.

Another kind of credit fix is to take care of financial problems such as budgeting and start to deal with concerns.

Significant Points to consider

- Credit repair is the action of repairing or restoring a bad credit rating.

  - Credit repair may also entail paying a company to get in touch with the credit agency and point out anything in your report that is untrue or incorrect, then requesting this to be eliminated.

You can do your own credit repair, but it may be time consuming and hard.

How Credit Repair Works

Though companies claim they are able to clean up credit reports that are poor, correcting requires time and energy. A third party cannot remove the information. The specifics, incorrect or if misrepresented can be contested. Individuals are eligible for free credit reports every 12 months in addition to if an action is taken against them. Disputes may be registered if incorrect or incomplete information appears in their credit reports. Besides correcting such advice, or grabbing fraudulent trades on one's Credit, fixing and rebuilding credit may break more heavily on credit use and credit action. The payment history of this person may be a factor in their own credit standing. Taking measures to make certain payments are current or enhance the payment program for outstanding credit may negatively impact their credit rating. The total amount of credit may play a role. As an example, if somebody is actively using huge parts of the credit available to them, even if they are keeping minimum payments in time, how big their debt they are taking could negatively affect their credit score. The matter is their liquidity might be driven by the debt. They could see improvements by taking steps to decrease their debt burden.

Chapter 2. Is Credit Repair Ethical?

Beware, not all credit repair companies are ethical. Do not fall for scams that promise they can take a bad credit record and turn it around overnight. Or that guarantee they can "force" the credit bureaus to remove all negative (but accurate) information from your credit file immediately. It takes time and your cooperation to improve your credit. Trust me when I tell you that a credit repair company cannot push around the large credit bureaus. Never mind order them to do things like immediately remove foreclosures or missed payments from the records of their client's. Inaccurate information can be easily fixed. However, removing accurate negative information takes a plan and is rarely done overnight. That usually requires filing official disputes, and careful negotiations with your creditors.

Some credit repair companies not only misrepresent what they can do for you, but also practice illegal or fraudulent ways of trying to improve your credit. Often, they will reorganize as a non-profit to get around state and federal laws that govern the industry. If you are desperate enough, you may be tempted to risk some of these illegal actions, but we would not recommend it. Also, be wary of credit repair companies that want to be paid up front. People have lost hundreds, and in some cases thousands of dollars to credit repair scams.

The Warning Signs When Choosing a Credit Repair Company

-They recommend that you do not contact credit bureaus directly.

-They do not disclose your legal rights or what you can do yourself.

-They want you to pay upfront based on their verbal promises before they do any work. It is illegal for them to charge you up front. They can only charge you after they have completed the services they contracted for.

-They suggest unethical or illegal actions such as making false statements on a loan application, misrepresenting your social security number, or obtaining an EIN number under false pretensions. The use of these tactics could constitute general fraud, civil fraud, mail fraud, wire fraud, and get you into a lot of trouble.

Basic of Credit Repair

By making your financial goals, setting your budget, finding ways to save money, and requesting a copy of your credit report, you have done your preliminary legwork in trying to get your finances back in order.

Now that all three credit reporting agencies have a copy of your credit report, it is time to roll up your sleeves and tackle the inaccurate information reported on your credit report.

Analyzing Your Credit Report

When you check each of your credit reports, whether it is on the website of the credit reporting agency where you can download it, or a hard copy of your report which you received in the mail, it is vital that each entry is accurately reported.

If the borrower fails to respond within that time period, the credit reporting agency must delete from the credit report the entry you are contesting. If the creditor replies and the inaccurate entry is corrected, the credit reporting agency will update your credit report. There is also the risk that the borrower can respond to the credit report and not make any changes in it. If you are not happy with your revised credit report, you should write a 100-word paragraph to clarify your side of the story on any of the remaining items on the credit report. This customer statement will then surface any time it appears on your credit report. If you do not want to write a 100-word paragraph on your credit report, you will be able to write another 120-day appeal letter from your most recent credit report.

The Disputing Process

The first thing you need to know is that all three credit reporting agencies have to contest the inaccurate information independently. The disputed appearance may be on all three credit reports or may not. Keep in mind that customers may not belong to all credit reporting agencies. This is why you will see that on one list some of the investors are not on the others.

Even though all three credit reporting agencies have the same information, this does not mean that if an item comes out of one credit report it will come out of the others. No promise is provided what the outcome will be. That is why you have to refute any inaccurate information about each particular article.

They can use their appeal forms when disputing with credit reporting agencies, write your own message, or challenge the item online on their Website. If you decide to dispute by letter-writing, simply state the facts in a simple, concise or two sentences. If you choose to write a personalized message, you can also use the same answers as appropriate. Sample answers would be:

- This is not my account.

- This was not late as indicated.

- This was not charged off.

- This was paid off in full as agreed.

- This was not a collection account.

- This is not my bankruptcy as indicated.

- This is not my tax lien as indicated.

- This is not my judgment as indicated.

If you have found more than four entries on your credit report that you need to dispute, do not dispute everything in one letter. Whether you are writing a letter, filling out their form or answering via the Internet, break your disputes. You send or go back every 30 days to the website of the credit reporting agency and challenge up to four more things. On submitting each address, expect to receive a revised credit report about 45 days after you send your letter or disagreement online. If your new credit report has not been issued before it is time to appeal the second time, go ahead and mail your second letter or challenge online instead.

Once all the grievance letters have been mailed or posted to their website and all the revised credit reports have been received, check whether products have been omitted or incomplete. If you need to do the procedure again for the remaining items, space 120 days from your most recent update for another disputes.

What you should not do:

- Alter your identity or try to change it.
- The story is fictional.
- Check any information which is 100% correct.

What you should do:

- Read your emails, should you decide to send them to us. If a letter looks legitimate, credit reporting agencies will believe it has been written by a credit repair service, and they will not investigate the dispute.
- Use your original letterhead (if you do have one).
- Use the appeal form included with the credit report by the credit reporting agency, if you want.
- Provide some evidence suggesting the wrong entry is erroneous.
- Include the identification number for all communications listed on the credit report.

Common Credit Report Errors

Note that there could be various mistakes in each of the three credit reports. It is not uncommon to have positive coverage of an account on one article, but poor reports on another.

Here are some of the most common credit report errors.

- Listed wrong names, emails, or phone numbers.
- Data that refers to another of the same name.
- Duplicate details, whether positive or negative, about the same account.
- Records have negative, apparently positive information.
- Balances on accounts payable are still on view.
- Delinquent payment reports that were never billed in due time.
- This indicates wrong credit limits.
- Claims included in the insolvency which are still due.
- Incorrect activity dates.
- Past-due payments not payable.
- Court records which are falsely connected with you, such as convictions and bankruptcy.
- Tax liens not yours.
- Unprecedented foreclosures.

Spotting Possible Identity Theft

Checking your credit report could also spot potential identity theft. That is why you should inquire at least once a year or every six months for a copy of your credit report.

Things to look for would be:

- Names of accounts and figures that you do not know.

- You do not remember filling out loan applications.

- Addresses you did not live in.

- Poor bosses or tenants' enquiries you do not know.

Creditors Can Help

Many times if you have had a long-term account with a creditor, you can contact them directly and explain the error being reported on your credit report.

Ask them to write you a letter with the email and correction. Also ask them to contact every credit reporting agency that reports this incorrect entry in order to make the correction.

Once the creditor receives a copy of the letter, make a copy of it, and attach the letter to the letter of dispute you send. Mail it to the agency for credit reporting and ask them to update their files. Once that is completed, you will be sent back a new credit report by the credit reporting agency.

Credit Rescoring

Rapid rescoring is an expedited way of fixing anomalies in the credit file of a customer. The bad news is you cannot do it yourself. A fast rescore dispute process works through borrowers and mortgage brokers, a number of approved registry credit reporting companies, and credit reporting agencies.

If you are a creditor applying for a rescore on your credit report, you would need to provide detailed documents that would be sent to the collateral agencies that are working on your case. Cash registry is the system used by cash grantors. The data archive gathers the records from the three main credit reporting agencies and has to check the consumer's initial information for a rescore. Once the verification is entered into the program of the repository a new score will be produced.

The key thing to keep in mind is that a simple rescore can only be temporary. You may be able to close a loan with it, but you must follow through on your credit report with the three main credit reporting firms to ensure it has been removed or corrected. If it reappears, forward the reports immediately to credit reporting agencies.

The downside of a fast rescore is that you save money without having to contend individually with a credit reporting agency that may take longer than 30 days to complete an audit. If the sale of a house or lease depends on your credit score, and you are in a time crunch, the best solution is to easily rescore.

First Step in Actually Repairing Your Credit

Write letters to the agencies with the correct but bad items you have encountered and your reasoning for which you think they should be taken off your credit report. The most important thing when writing these letters and when making any type of contact with the people at the credit report agencies is to keep communication very polite and professional. The more pleasant and prepared you are, the more you increase the chances of them helping you repair your credit. Sign and date your letters and try to write them by hand.

Contact with The Creditor

At this point, you have to write another letter, this time to the creditor. You can continue claiming that the negative information is wrong but be warned that they will not believe you if you do not provide solid proof to back up your claim. If you do not think you can muster up that proof in order to make a good case for re-establishing your good credit.

Chapter 3. Self-Credit Repair Step

Step 1: Know your credit score

First things first, see what your credit score is and check your credit report. Most people will tell you that you can check your credit report for free once a year by visiting www.AnnualCreditReport.com. This report will not tell you your credit score. Also, if you are trying to fix your credit score, you will need to check your report at least once a month, not once a year. Other people might also direct you to sources that charge you for checking your credit score or that hurt your credit score every time you check it. Do not do that.

Following is a list of FREE resources where you can check your credit score without having to worry about it costing a thing or hurting your credit:

- www.creditkarma.com – use this site when fixing your credit score. The site provides free credit reports and scores from Equifax and Transunion that are updated every week.

- www.creditsesame.com - Same as credit karma but updates every month instead of week. It gives you a free credit score, but not a free credit report.

- www.quizzle.com - offers a free credit report and score every 3 months.

- www.credit.com - You get two free credit reports and your score is updated once a month.

- www.wallethub.com - gives daily updates to its free credit scores and reports. There are some more websites out there, but these are the most popular.

Once you have signed up with one of these sites and checked your credit score, it is time to analyze your credit report for errors.

Step 2: Thoroughly scan your credit report

Everyone has three credit reports: one from Experian, one from Equifax, and one from Transunion. These are the three big credit bureaus.

Once you get your free report, thoroughly go over it. Is everything correct? Remember, it is actually quite common for mistakes to be on your credit report. It is very important for you to highlight any errors these should be removed from your report, which will increase your credit score

Here are some questions to ask yourself when you go through your record: Are all of my accounts listed? Is my personal information correct? Are all missed and/or late payments correctly listed? Is there anything I do not recognize? Are there still accounts listed that are decades-old? Go over every single thing.

Step 3: Fixing errors on your credit report

First, go over all missed/late payments. Check if you recognize it. If not, dispute it. Have you paid it already? Dispute it. Is the payment more than 7 years old? Dispute it. Other people are inclined to tell you that you need to pay your missed payments and collections so you can just be done with it.

Then check the inquires done on your credit. Dispute any incorrect or unauthorized inquires. Same goes for collections and public records. This is one of the secrets of fixing bad credit. Before disputing, make sure that you are not disputing something that is positively influencing your credit score. Only dispute personal information, credit inquiries, charge offs, collections, bankruptcies, foreclosures, repossessions, tax liens, judgments and others.

But how exactly do you dispute a charge? For every error, you need to dispute it by all three credit bureaus. I suggest writing them a letter via postal mail, but nowadays you can also dispute charges online. The problem with filing a dispute online is that oftentimes, you agree to not being able to sue them if the charge is not removed. You limit your rights, giving you less control and making the process less effective.

Also, do not dispute via phone. You need evidence and records of your dispute. You can easily find a sample letter which you can send to the credit bureaus. All the credit bureaus also have their own dispute letter form, just check their website. Print and mail the dispute letter along with ID and proof of address. Always keep a copy of the letter for your records and request a return receipt via post. The credit bureaus legally have 30 days to act on the notice.

Step 4: Passed Payment History

Your past payment history has the biggest impact. Fix any late payments and avoid late payments in the future. What you can do is setting up payment due alerts and becoming more organized. If the due dates are inconsistent with the dates you get paid, talk with your bank or lender to change the payment date. If you get paid at the end of every month, change your due date to the end of every month too. If fixing any late payments is hard, request the issuer or lender if they can forgive the charge. Tell them that you were out on vacation, the check got lost via the mail, or you did not get notice of the bill and did not know it existed. Some issuers, especially credit card issuers, are pretty soft-hearted if you have had a strong track record of making payments in the past. What is worse than having a bad payment history, is having no payment history. If you have no payment history, try getting a secured credit card and making on-time payments in order to build up a healthy payment history. Really try to pay your bills on time in the future.

Step 5: Debt-to-Credit Ratio

Keep the balances low. You should use only a small portion of the credit available to you. Avoid maxing out. You could make all your payments on time, but it is also essential to keep your balance low when it comes to your credit card, or any revolving credit account for that matter. Credit cards are the main weight of debt-ratio rates, so if you do not have a credit card, definitely get one. To figure out your credit card's debt-ratio, divide your credit card balance by your available credit line. So if you spent $200 out of your $1000 credit line, that's 200/1000=0.2, which is 20%. This is good. FICO recommends a debt-to-credit ratio to be under 30%. If your debt-to-credit ratio is at or above 30%, decrease your spending or increase your credit line, your bank will likely agree to increasing your credit line.

Step 6: Negotiate your existing accounts

If you have open accounts that are severely delinquent, showing late payments or slow payments contact the creditor(s) and try to negotiate a new payment arrangement.

- Ask for more time to pay-off the loan; consider this, if you have a 36 months term loan ask if it can be extended to 42 months

- Ask for a lower interest rate?

- Ask what are your options?

You can do this yourself without the help of those companies and organizations that try to put you on a special payment plan charging lots of money to do something you can do for yourself. This is extra money that can be used to pay off some of that debt. Simply explain to the creditor(s) you are having financial difficulties, below are some typical hardships:

- going through a divorce

- getting sick and being under-insured or no medical insurance

- death of a close relative (parent, sibling, spouse, child)

- losing a job or job cutting back on hours
- a major car repairs (replace engine/transmission)
- car accident
- becoming disabled
- a run of bad luck, etcetera

Remember to notate your schedule on all the progress you have made negotiating your payoffs.

Chapter 4. The Debt Snowball

Before you can start paying off your debt, it is important to come up with a plan for debt repayment. If you have just one debt to worry about, then the best strategy is to start repaying as much as you can every month. You must keep doing this until you are debt-free.

If you are like a lot of others who are in debt, then you might have multiple debts. You must try to come up with the best repayment strategy which appeals to you and works well for your financial situation.

One method for repaying your debts is known as the debt snowball. You start repaying your debts in ascending order- starting from the smallest amount to the largest one. As you start clearing small loans, it will give you the motivation to keep going. You can start enjoying your small wins as you make your way to being debt-free.

You must start paying the minimum balance due on all your debts. Once you do this, divert all your extra funds toward the debt with the smallest amount. Once you clear this debt, all the money you were spending on this repayment can be diverted towards the small debt on your list. Keep doing this until you paid off all your debts. Regardless of the rates of interest payable, you must start with the smallest sum due and make your way to the largest one. If you ever played in the snow and made a snowball, you will realize that as the snowball rolls on the ground, it keeps collecting more and more snow and becomes bigger. So, every small debt you repay will free up sufficient funds to repay the debt.

Let us assume that you have four debts, and their details are as follows:

- An auto loan repayable at 4.5% for $16,000.
- A student loan repayable at 6.5% for $30,000.
- A personal loan repayable at 8% for $10,000.
- A credit card debt repayable at 21% for $7000.

So, you will start by repaying your credit card debt, which is at $7000. Once you repay this diet and have paid the minimum balance due for all the other loans. All the interest which was payable towards the credit card debt can be successfully redirected toward the payment of the other loans. So, you will start with your credit card debt, then the personal loan, auto loan, and then finally the student loan.

This is a great technique to pay your debts, especially if you have several small debts. At times, it can be rather overwhelming and scary when you look at a major debt. It can also be the reason for losing your motivation. To avoid this, when you start clearing the small debts, the number of loans you have to repay will reduce. If you have five loans, and you repay two loans, the figure somehow looks more manageable. Instead of worrying about repaying all the five loans at the same time, you can concentrate on repaying the smallest ones, and then be left with only the major debts.

How debt snowball method works:

Step 1: List the debts from lowest to highest.

Stage 2: Make minimum payments on all but the smallest debts

Stage 3: Follow this process with as you clear all your debt. The more you pay off, the more your freed-up money grows it is like a snowball going downhill.

What You Should Include in Your Debt Snowball?

Your debt snowball should include all non-mortgage debt, a loan that is described as anything else you owe to anyone.

- Car notes
- Credit card balances
- Home equity loans
- Medical bills
- Payday loans
- Personal loans
- Student loans

When compared to the Avalanche method, by using the snowball method, you might end up paying more interest in the long run. Since the interest rates are never taken into consideration in this method, any account, which has a higher rate of interest and a large outstanding balance, will be left towards the end. So, the interest payable will obviously increase.

Chapter 5. What Is Section 609

Basically, a 609 is known as a dispute letter, which you would send to your creditor if you saw you were overcharged or unfairly charged. Most people use a 609 letter in order to get the information they feel they should have received. There are several reasons why some information might be kept from you.

A section 609 letter is sent after two main steps. First, you see that the dispute is on your credit report. Second, you have already filed and processed a debt validation letter. The basis of the letter is that you will use it in order to take unfair charges off of your credit report, which will then increase your credit score.

The 609 letters can easily help you delete your bad credit. Other than this, there are a couple of other benefits you will receive from the letter. One of these benefits is that you will obtain your documentation and information as the credit bureau has to release this information to you. Secondly, you will be able to obtain an accurate credit report, which can definitely help you increase your credit score.

There are also disadvantages to the 609 letters. One of these disadvantages is that collection agencies can add information to your credit history at any time. A second disadvantage is that you still have to repay debt. You cannot use the 609 letters in order to remove debt that you are obligated to pay. Finally, your creditor can do their own investigation and add the information back into your credit report, even if it was removed (Irby, 2019).

One of the reasons section 609 came to be is because one of five people state they have inaccurate information on the credit report (Black, 2019). At the same time many people believe that this statistic is actually higher than 20 percent of Americans.

How Section 609 Works to Repair Bad Credit

If you notice anything on your report that should not be there, you need to use the section 609 loophole in order to file a dispute, which could result in their wrong information being taken off of the report. If this is the case, your credit score will increase as you will no longer have this negative inaccuracy affecting your score.

How to File a Dispute with Section 609

It is important to note that there are several template letters for section 609. What this means is that you can easily download and use one of these templates yourself. While you usually have to pay for them, there are some which are free. Of course, you will want to remember to include your information in the letter before you send it.

You will want to make sure everything is done correctly as this will make it more likely that the information will come off and no one will place it back on your report again.

1. Find a dispute letter through googling "section 609 dispute letter". While you might be able to find a free download, for some, you will be able to copy and paste into Microsoft Word or onto a Google Doc.

2. Make the necessary changes to the letter. This will include changing the name and address. You will also want to make sure your phone number is included. Sometimes people include their email address, but this is not necessary. In fact, it is always safer to only include your home address or PO box information. You will also want to make sure to edit the whole letter. If something does not match up to what you want to say in your letter,

such as what you are trying to dispute on your credit report, you need to state this. These letters are quite generic, which means you need to add in your own information.

3. You want to make sure that all of your account information you want to be taken off your credit report is handwritten. You also want to make sure you use blue ink rather than black. On top of this, you do not need to worry about being too neat, but you want to make sure they can read the letters and numbers correctly. This is an important part of filing your dispute letter because handwritten ones in blue ink will not be pushed through their automated system. They have an automatic system which will read the letter for them and punch in the account number you use. They will then send you a generic letter that states these accounts are now off your credit report, which does not mean that it actually happened. When you write the information down, a person needs to read it and will typically take care of it. Of course, this does not mean that you will not be pushed aside. Unfortunately, this can happen with any letters.

4. You want to make sure that you prove who you are with your letters. While this is never a comfortable thing

to do, you must send a copy of your social security card and your driver's license or they will shred your letter. You also need to make sure that you get each of your letters notarized. You can typically do this by visiting your county's courthouse.

5. You can send as many letters as you need to; however, keep in mind that the creditor typically will not make you send more than four. This is because when you threaten to take them to court in the third letter, they will realize that your accounts and demands just are not worth it. First, you could damage their reputation, and secondly, you will cost them more money than simply taking the information off of your credit report will.

6. You will want to make sure that you keep all correspondence they send you. This will come in handy when they try to make you send more information or keep telling you that they cannot do anything. It is important that you do not give up. Many people struggle to get them to pay attention because that is just how the system works. Therefore, you need to make sure that you do not listen to their quick automatic reply that your information is off of your credit report. You also want to make sure to wait at least three months and then re-run

your credit report to make sure the wrong information has been removed. Keep track of every time you need to re-run your credit report as you can use this as proof if they continue to send you a letter stating the information is off of your credit report.

It is important to note that you can now file a dispute letter online with all three credit bureaus. However, this is a new system, which means that it does come with more problems than sending one through the mail. While it is completely your choice whether you use a form to file your 609 dispute or send a letter, you always want to make sure you keep copies and continue to track them, even if you don't hear from the credit bureau after a couple of months. It will never hurt to send them a second letter or even a third.

What Are My Rights Under 609?

The Fair Credit Reporting Act is going to cover a lot of the aspects and the components of credit checking to make sure that it is able to maintain a reasonable amount of privacy and accuracy along the way. This agency is going to list all of the responsibilities that credit reporting companies and any credit bureaus will have, and it also includes the rights of the consumer which will be your rights in this situation. This Act is going to be the part that will govern how everything is going to work to ensure that all parties are treated in a fair manner.

When using this act the consumer has to be told if any of the information that is on your file has been in the past or is now being used against you in any way, shape, or form. You have a right to know whether the information is harming you and what that information is.

In addition, the consumer is going to have the right to go through and dispute any information that may be seen as inaccurate or incomplete at the time. If they see that there are items in the documents they are sent, if the billing to them is not right or there is something else off in the process, the consumer has the right to dispute this and the credit reporting agency needs to at least look into it and determine if the consumer is right.

This Act is going to limit the access that third parties can have to your file. You personally have to go through and provide your consent before someone is able to go through and look at your credit score, whether it is a potential employer or another institution providing you with funding.

They are not able to get in and just look at it. Keep in mind that if you do not agree for them to take a look at the information, it is going to likely result in you not getting the funding that you want, because there are very few ways that the institution can fairly assess the risk that you pose to them in terms of creditworthiness.

it means that you may have debt or another negative item that is on your credit report, but there is a way to get around this without having to wait for years to get that to drop off your report or having to pay back a debt that you are not able to afford.

Keep in mind that this is not meant to be a method for you to take on a lot of debts that you cannot afford and then just dump them. But on occasion, there could be a few that you are able to fight and get an instant boost to your credit score in the process.

Why Use a 609 Letter?

The 609 Letter is going to be one of the newest credit repair secrets that will help you to remove a lot of information on your credit report, all of the false information and sometimes even the accurate information, thanks to a little loophole that is found in our credit reporting laws. You can use this kind of letter in order to resolve some of the inaccuracies that show up, to dispute your errors, and handle some of the other items that could inaccurately come in and impact and lower your credit score.

Using these 609 letters is a good way for us to clean up our credit a bit and in some cases, it is going to make a perfect situation. However, we have to remember that outside of some of the obvious benefits that we are going to discuss, there are a few things that we need to be aware of ahead of time.

There are few limitations that are going to come with this as well, for example, even after you work with the 609 letters, it is possible that information that is seen as accurate could be added to the report again, even after the removal. This is going to happen if the creditor is able to verify the accuracy. They may take it off for a bit if the 30 days have passed and they are not able to verify at that point. But if the information is accurate, remember that it could end up back on the report.

Chapter 6. General Advice to See Success With 609

It is important to gain as much information as possible so you can write the best letter. While you might not care to do this when it comes to the credit bureau, they often pay more attention to letters that are done professionally. Furthermore, many letters are placed to the side because the customer did not include all the information or correct documentation.

These are not only tips detailing the information you should put into your dispute letter, but they are also tipping from people who have successfully used the 609 loopholes to repair their credit.

Include Documentation

When it comes to your dispute letter, it is important to remember that documentation is key. There are two factors that go into making sure you provide proof. First, this makes your case that what is written on your credit report is wrong. Even though the credit bureau still has up to 90 days to investigate your claims, making sure to send documentation is going to result in your case being even stronger. Furthermore, it proves that you completely understand what this wrong information is doing to your credit report and that you intend to fix this, which is your right provided by section 609.

You want to include as much documentation as you need to. This means that you can send a copy of your credit report, including highlighting the information that it wrong. At the same time, you need to make sure that the information is also handwritten in your letter. Enclosing a copy of your credit reports simply proves that this information is truly on your report and it is not made up.

You also want to make sure that you include the information to verify that you really are yourself. If copies of your identification card, such as a state-issued ID or driver's license along with your social security card are not enclosed, they might not take any action with your letter. The fact is that this letter could have been written and sent by anyone.

You also want to make sure that you send any copies of checks, credit card receipts, and any correspondence. This means that if you are sending your second letter to the credit bureau, you should also include your first letter.

Never send originals to the credit bureau. You always want to make sure that you send copies and keep the originals for yourself.

Be Thorough

You want to make sure you are concise with your information but also thorough. This might mean that you spend a good amount of time writing your letter. It is important that you keep it about a page in length, make sure that everything is readable, and you do not make the print to small. The best font to use is Times New Roman and the best size to use is 12-point font. This is standard when it comes to business letters. You do not need to pick the fun font as this is not meant to be a fun and interesting letter; it is meant to be straight to the point and to provide all the information necessary.

The trick is to simply state the facts, such as what is wrong and what you want to happen so the issue is resolved. You do not really need to explain why you think it is wrong, but you need to explain what the situation is.

Illustrate Your Case

You want to make sure that you explain what about the information you believe to be wrong. You do not just want to say that certain information on your credit report is wrong and you would like it removed and then list the incorrect information. You want to make sure that you give them information that makes you prove it is wrong in a written way. You will want to give them the numbers for the incorrect information, which will be shown on your credit report, and then move on to the other item or finish the letter. You will then want to include documentation proving that you made these payments.

Proofread the Letter Thoroughly

You do not want to be in so much of a hurry to send this letter that you spell something incorrectly. This is going to reflect negatively on you. Even though misspellings happen, this is a short and simple letter that will not take longer than a few minutes to edit.

It is important to not just read the words but also to make sure all the numbers are correct. It is common for people to mix up a couple of digits when there is a long series of numbers.

Proofreading your letter will also help you make sure that you have all the necessary information but did not become too detailed. If you do not feel comfortable proofreading your own letter, take it to a friend or family member to look at it.

You can also match up your information with the templates online to make sure you have everything that you need in the letter.

Get Advice If Necessary

If you want to make sure that you are reading your credit report correctly or you want to get reassurance that you are correct, you can seek advice from a professional. You do not have to contact an attorney; you can simply go to your financial advisor or someone else you trust for help. For example, loan advisors at banks regularly read credit reports and might be willing to help you, especially if you have a relationship with the banker.

Of course, there is also a lot of advice that you can find online. There are a lot of people who share their stories of writing letters and are willing to help you with anything you need to make sure that you get all incorrect information taken off your report.

What Not to Disclose in Your Letter

It is just as important to make sure that you do not disclose certain information.

First, you never want to disclose what you do not want to dispute. This means that you do not want to place anything in your letter that is correctly on your credit report. Some people will often scan their credit report and black out the other information that the credit bureau does not need to see with the letter. They might do this in order to highlight what is wrong or for their own protection.

Secondly, unless you have a legitimate reason to do so and you have gotten advice from an attorney, you do not want to threaten legal action. This can be okay to do by the time you are sending your third letter. However, you always want to make sure to get legal advice before you threaten to sue anyone. This is just an extra step to make sure that you do not cross any legal lines that you are unaware of.

Third, you do not want to dispute any credit card payments that you fell behind on recently. There is a statute of limitations, which means that if you did not make the last two payments on a credit card that states you didn't make two payments last year, when you know you did, leave this dispute out. Because you are currently behind, this will reflect negatively on you and it can have your whole case thrown out.

Finally, there are ways that you can dispute over the phone or online. However, it is advised that you never do this. One of the main reasons you do not want to do this is you are not allowed to keep copies of correspondence. While you never want to end up going to court over this claim, and it is rare that this happens, you always want to act like this could happen. Another reason is that when you try to dispute over the phone, you need to verbally agree to certain terms. These are often stated in a very confusing way. One of the most common agreements made over the phone that you would never agree to on paper is to waive any right to a reinvestigation. This means that if the credit bureau states nothing could be found to support your claim, you cannot try to reopen the case. In general, disputing online or over the phone is a huge disadvantage for you.

Make Sure Everything Is Readable

No matter what you send, you want to make sure that someone else will be able to read it. This is another reason why someone having proofread your letter is often the best option as they will be able to tell you if something is not readable or does not make sense.

While you should do your best to type as much information as possible, you should not write the letter by hand. While this will be accepted, it is generally not something that people do in this day and age. Furthermore, typing most of the information will ensure that words are not mistaken for another word, which can happen with handwriting. While you might feel your handwriting is easily readable, someone else might not be able to understand it as well.

Do not Bypass the Credit Reporting Agency

Some people feel that having to write a dispute letter to the credit bureau is the long road. Instead, they want to direct it to the lender. This is a common mistake that people make and one that can make the process longer than it initially is.

Another reason people often go directly to the lender is that section 609 states that you can do this. However, this also makes it, so you have more difficulty fighting your case. Chances are that the lender is not going to fix the mistake very easily. If you find that you need to take stronger measures, you could have a bigger struggle on your hands because you did not contact the credit bureau first.

Chapter 7. How to Proceed with The Letters

Before we get started here, there are a few tips and rules that we need to follow in order to make sure that we are going to get the most out of the templates that we want to use. We are going to take a look at a number of different letters and templates that we are able to send out to the agencies that report our credit so that we can dispute some of the debt or the negative items that are on our reports. All of these are going to be easy to tailor and will talk about Section 609 to make it a bit easier for you.

These templates will help you compose and keep your dispute as organized as possible. When you pay attention to some of the details that are there, you are going to find that it is easier to come up with a letter that is convincing and effective.

There are a few different ways that we are able to make sure these letters get back to the right parties, and we are going to take a look at all of them below:

Emails

Our world seems to run online all the time and finding ways to work on our credit scores and not have to waste a lot of time copying things or worrying about the paper trails can seem like a great idea. And in some cases, we may find that sending in our 609 letters through email is going to be the best situation for our needs.

Before you do this, though, make sure that you take the time and do the proper research. You want the forms to end up in the right locations, rather than getting sent to the wrong departments, and not doing anything for you in the process. Most of the time there will be listings for the various departments that you want to handle and work with for each credit agency, so take a look at those.

Again, when you are ready, you need to have as many details ready to go for this as possible. Just sending in a few lines about the process and thinking that will get things done is foolish. Write out a letter just like you would if you planned to send these by mail and use that as the main body of your email. Mention Section 609 and some of the disputes that you want to bring up.

In addition to this, you need to take some time adding in the other details. Attach some ways to prove your identity to the email, along with a copy of the credit report that has been highlighted to show what is going on and what you would like to dispute. Add in any of the other documentation that is needed to help support your case, and have it as clean and organized as possible to make sure the right people can find it and will utilize this information to help you out.

Doing it All Online

Many of the credit agencies have made it easier to go through and work on some of these claims online. This helps you out because you will not need to go through and print it all off or worry about finding the paperwork or printing a bunch of things off. And if you are already on your credit report, your identification has been taken care of.

Since so many people are online these days, doing this right from the credit report is a simple and easy process to work with, and you will catch onto it fairly quickly. Do not take the easy way out with this. If you just click on the part that you think is wrong and submit a claim on it, this is not enough. There will not be any reference back to Section 609, and you will not be able to get them to necessarily follow the rules that come with Section 609.

This is where being detailed is going to be useful in the long run. When you do submit one of these claims online, make sure that you write a note with it to talk about Section 609, specifically the part of 609 that you want to reference in this dispute. You can usually attach other forms to document who you are and why you think these need to be dropped.

Treat this just like you would if you tried to mail the information to the credit agency. The more details that you are able to include in this, the better. This will help to build up your case and can make it harder for those items to stay on your credit report for a long period of time. Make sure to mention the 30-day time limit as well.

Telephone

A telephone is one method that you can use, but it is not usually the right one for this kind of process. For example, how easy is it going to be to show the credit agency what your driver's license looks like? You can repeat the number over if you would like, but this process is still a bit more laborious than some of the others and does not always work as well as we would hope it could.

However, this is definitely an option that we can use in order to reach the credit agencies, and for some people who are not sure of what their rights are, or would rather talk directly to the individuals in charge about this issue, the telephone can be the right option. Make sure that you have a copy of your credit report in front of you when you start and having some other identification information and more. This will ensure that you are prepared when someone comes on the line to speak with you.

There is the possibility that the other side is going to have some questions for you, and they will at least want to go through and verify your identity to make sure they are ready to go. But the same rules apply here, and if you do not get a response within 30 days of that phone call, then the information should be erased.

Keep good records of the conversation, who you talked to during that time, what time and date it was, and so on. This will make it easier to get someone to respond to you and can help us to get this to work in our favor. Also, remember that you will need to repeat these phone calls to all three credit bureaus in order to get your information cleared on all of them.

Mail

Another option that you are able to work with is mail. This is usually a good method to use because it allows you a way to send in all of the information at once. Since you probably already have a physical copy of your SSN, driver's license, the credit report and more, you can get copies of these made pretty quickly, and then send them on with the Section 609 letter that you are working with. This method also allows us a way to go through and circle or highlight the parts of our credit report that we want to point out to the credit reporting agency.

This method is quick and efficient and will make sure that the information gets to the right party. You can try some of the other options, but sometimes this brings up issues like your information getting lost in the spam folder or getting sent to the wrong part. Mail can take some of that out of the way and will ensure that everything gets to the right location at the right time.

Certified Mail

For the most part, you are going to find that working with certified mail is going to be one of the best options that you can choose. This will ensure that the letter gets to the right place and can tell you for certain when the 30-day countdown is going to begin.

If you send this with regular mail, you have to make some guesses on when the letter will arrive at the end address that you want. And sometimes you will be wrong. If there is a delay in the mailing and it gets there too late, then you may start your 30 days too early. On the other hand, if you assume it is going to take so many days and it takes less, you may wait around too long and miss your chance to take this loophole and use it to your advantage.

Certified mail is able to fix this issue. When the credit agency receives the letter, you will get a receipt about that exact date and even the time. This is going to make it so much easier for you to have exact times, and you can add these to your records. There is no more guessing along the way, and you can be sure that this particular loophole is going to work to your advantage.

Another benefit that comes with certified mail is that you make sure that it gets to its location. If you never get a receipt back or get something back that says the letter was rejected or not left at the right place, then you will know about this ahead of time. On the other hand, if it does get to its location, you will know this and have proof of it.

Sometimes things get lost. But you want to be on the winning side of that one. If the credit agency says that they did not receive the letter, you will have proof that you sent it and that someone within the business received it and signed for it. Whether the company lost it along the way, or they are trying to be nefarious and not fix the issue for you, the certified mail will help you to get it to all work for you.

When it comes to worrying about those 30 days and how it will affect you, having it all in writing and receipts to show what you have done and when is going to be important. This can take out some of the guesswork in the process and will ensure that you are actually going to get things to work for you if the 30 days have come and gone, and no one will be able to come back and say that you didn't follow the right procedures.

As we can see, there are a few different options that we are able to use when it comes to sending out our Section 609 letters.

Chapter 8. The Templates You Need (609 Letter)

LETTER #1

(INITIAL LETTER TO Credit Bureau disputing items)

{Name of Bureau}

{Address}

{Date}

{Name on account}

{Report number}

To whom it may concern:

On {Date of Credit Report} I received a copy of my credit report which contains errors that are damaging to my credit score. I am requesting the following items be completely investigated as each account contains several mistakes.

{Creditor 1 / Account number}

{Creditor 2 / Account number}

{Creditor 3 / Account number}

Thank you in advance for your time. I understand that you need to check with the original creditors on these accounts and that you will make sure every detail is accurate. I also understand that under the Fair Credit Reporting Act you will need to complete your investigation within 30 days of receiving this letter. Once you are finished with your investigation, please send me a copy of my new credit report showing the changes. I look forward to hearing from you as I am actively looking for a new job and would not want these mistakes on my credit report to stand in my way.

Sincerely,

{Your signature}

{Your Printed Name}

{Your Address}

{Your Phone Number}

{Your Social Security Number}

Include a copy of the credit report showing which accounts you are disputing

LETTER #2

(When you do not get a response from Letter #1)

{Name of Bureau}

{Address}

{Date}

{Name on account}

{Report number}

To whom it may concern:

On {Date of your first letter} I sent you a letter asking you to investigate several mistakes on my credit report. I have included a copy of my first letter and a copy of the report with the mistakes circled. The Fair Credit Reporting Act says I should only have to wait 30 days for the investigation to be finished. It has been more than 30 days and I still have not heard anything.

I am guessing that since you have not responded that you were not able to verify the information on the mistaken accounts. Since it has been more than 30 days, please remove the mistakes from my credit report and send me a copy of my updated credit report. Also, as required by law, please send an updated copy of my credit report to anyone who requested a copy of my credit file in the past six months.

I look forward to hearing from you as I am actively looking for a new job and would not want these mistakes on my credit report to stand in my way.

Sincerely,

{Your signature}

{Your Printed Name}

{Your Address}

{Your Phone Number}

{Your Social Security Number}

Include a copy of the credit report showing which accounts you are disputing

Include a copy of your original letter

Include a copy of the registered letter receipts showing the date they received your original letter

LETTER #3

(Request for removal of negative items from original creditor)

{Name of Creditor}

{Address}

{Date}

{Name on account}

To whom it may concern:

On {Date of Credit Report} I received a copy of my credit report which contains errors that are damaging to my credit score. I am requesting the following items be completely investigated as each account contains several mistakes.

{Description of item(s) you are disputing/account number(s)}

I have included a copy of the credit report and have highlighted the account(s) in question.

Thank you in advance for your time. I understand that you need to check on these accounts and that you will make sure every detail is accurate. I also understand that under the Fair Credit Reporting Act you will need to complete your investigation within 30 days of receiving this letter. Once you are finished with your investigation, please alert all major credit bureaus where you have reported my information. Also, please send me a letter confirming the changes.

I look forward to hearing from you as I am actively looking for a new job and would not want these mistakes on my credit report to stand in my way.

Sincerely,

{Your signature}

{Your Printed Name}

{Your Address}

{Your Phone Number}

{Your Social Security Number}

Include a copy of the credit report showing which accounts you are disputing

LETTER #4

(If you do not receive a response from Letter #3)

{Name of Creditor}

{Address}

{Date}

{Name on account}

To whom it may concern:

On {Date of your first letter} I sent you a letter asking you to investigate several mistakes on my credit report. I have included a copy of my first letter and a copy of the report with the mistakes circled. The Fair Credit Reporting Act says I should only have to wait 30 days for the investigation to be finished. It has been more than 30 days and I still have not heard anything.

I am guessing that since you have not responded that you were not able to verify the information on the mistaken accounts. Since it has been more than 30 days, please immediately report the updated information to all major credit bureaus so they may update my credit report. Also, please send me a letter confirming these changes to the way you report my account.

I look forward to hearing from you as I am actively looking for a new job and would not want these mistakes on my credit report to stand in my way.

Sincerely,

{Your signature}

{Your Printed Name}

{Your Address}

{Your Phone Number}

{Your Social Security Number}

Include a copy of the credit report showing which accounts you are disputing

Include a copy of your original letter

Include a copy of the registered letter receipts showing the date they received your original letter

LETTER #5

(If the Credit Bureau does not remove negative items disputed)

{Name of Credit Bureau}

{Address}

{Date}

{Name on account}

{Report number}

To whom it may concern:

On {Date of your first letter} I sent you a letter asking you to investigate several mistakes on my credit report. I have included a copy of my first letter and a copy of the report with the mistakes circled. According to your response you have chosen to leave these negative items on my credit report adding insult to injury. The items in question are:

{Creditor 1 / Account number}

{Creditor 2 / Account number}

{Creditor 3 / Account number}

I find it completely unacceptable that you and the creditor refuse to properly investigate my dispute. Your refusal to follow the Fair Credit Reporting Act is causing me untold stress and anxiety. Since you will not follow through, I want to know exactly how you investigated each account. Therefore, I would like the name, title, and contact information for the person at the creditor with whom you did the investigation. This will allow me to personally follow up with the creditor and find out why they are choosing to report these mistakes on my credit month after month.

I know I am only one person among thousands or more that you have to look after, but to me this is both personally damaging and humiliating. You may not understand it and you do not have to--all I am asking is that when people look at my credit file, they see the most accurate information and that is not what is happening.

Please provide me with the requested information right away so I can finally put this nightmare behind me.

I look forward to hearing from you as I am actively looking for a new job and would not want these mistakes on my credit report to stand in my way.

Sincerely,

{Your signature}

{Your Printed Name}

{Your Address}

{Your Phone Number}

{Your Social Security Number}

Include a copy of the credit report showing which accounts you are disputing

Include a copy of your original letter

Include a copy of the Bureau's response showing no changes to your credit

Chapter 9. How to Boost Your Credit Score 100+ Points?

If you are trying to improve your credit score as quickly as possible, ask for a free copy of your credit report and check it as soon as possible. You need to know what is in your credit report before you can find out what you need to do to change it.

Check the credit report

The credit score provides a snapshot of your credit status and is determined by a series of factors that can be divided into the following categories: credit history - How long have you been using credit?

Payment History

Do you have a history of paying on time?

Credit amount - How much do you do and how much do you owe?

Check over your credit report with a fine-tooth comb: verify that the amount due for each account is accurate. And look for all the accounts you paid off that still show as outstanding issues. Pay particular attention to any requests for recent information that you have not authorized. Before an endorsing creditor, or someone pretending to be you, for an account, they will make a request that will be indicated on your credit report.

Checking your credit report on a regular basis, at least once a year, is a good way to collect any cases where you could be the target of identity theft - or the credit bureau has accidentally mixed your story with someone similar name.

Pay early and often (or at least, on time)
Credit reports record payment habits on all types of bills and extended credit, not just credit cards. And sometimes these objects show up on their own official report, but not that of another. Old, unpaid gymnastic odds that only appear on a relationship could be affecting your score without even realizing it.

A full one-third of your score depends on whether you pay your creditors on time. So, make sure you pay all your bills by their due dates, including rent/mortgage, utilities, doctor's bills, etc. Keep documentation (such as checks or canceled receipts) to be able to prove that you have done the punctuality of payments.

The Fair Isaac Corporation, which calculates FICO scores, recommends signing up for payment notices if the lender makes them available. You will receive an email or text message announcing the upcoming expiration date, making it more difficult to forget a payment. Another approach is to create automatic drafts from your bank account.

Pick up a payment order
When using your cards, try to pay them off as soon as you can (you do not need to wait for the instruction in the mail, but you can pay online at any time). When you have the extra money to pay your balances, focus on the cards that are closest to being maxed out, to benefit your most credit score. Zero in credit card balances that are over 50% of your credit limit. Borrowers who have used up more of their available credit are considered higher risk.

Do not open too many accounts

The number of credit accounts you have opened is also important for control. Credit cards are easy to open. Almost every store has a quick, convenient way to get a new card. interesting incentives, such as discounts on the purchases of the day you sign up, add to the temptation. If you shop at that store, it can often be worth getting your card; otherwise, resist the temptation.

What is more, every time you apply for credit the potential lender will check your score. Whenever the credit is selected, other potential lenders worry about the additional debt that they can take on. Sometimes, the act of opening a new account, or even applying for one, can lower the score; have a lot of recent inquiries about your credit report dings your score temporarily. So do not ask for the card often if you want to increase your credit score.

Do not close credit cards

A good idea would be to keep three or four credit card accounts open but use only one or two of them; put away or cut the others. Once you have paid a card, however, keep the account open, even if you do not want to use it anymore. Closing a credit card will lower your credit score, even if it is always paid on time and I have not had a balance. The credit card company will report to the credit bureau that you have a good record with them, which will increase your credit rating.

In closing, late accounts or those with a history of late payments can also help, as long as you have paid them in full. Because history is important if you decide to close a couple of accounts, close the most recent ones. The length of your credit history is 15% of your score, so even after paying the sales down, keep the oldest cards open. Be sure to use these cards to make occasional purchases (so pay the bills in full), so the card company does not close the account due to inactivity.

Increase the credit limit

There is a way to increase your credit score that does not involve paying a debt or any of the other more traditional credit score tactics by increasing. Since credit scores are determined, in part, on the difference between the credit limit and the amount of credit used, ask for a higher credit limit. Your chances of increasing it are probably better than you think. Of those applying for a higher credit limit, 8 out of 10 have been approved, according to a recent money survey. While it helps to be over 30, there is a good chance for all adults. To prevent the credit decreased with the request for a higher limit, to ask for the highest credit line increase that does not trigger what is called a difficult request.

By increasing the credit limit, the differential between the amount you are allowed to borrow and the amount you actually make is automatically increased. The larger the spread, the higher the credit score.

The credit utilization report

This spread, known as the credit utilization ratio, is expressed as a percentage. For example, if the limit on the MasterCard is $ 5,000 and you have a budget of $ 4,000, the usage ratio is 80%. If you request a credit line increase and the limit goes up to $ 10,000, suddenly your use is only 40%.

Obviously, the higher the percentage, the worse you look. Experts have long said that using 30% of available credit is a good way to keep your credit score high. More recently, this recommendation has been reduced to 20%. In the $ 5000 MasterCard limit example above, 30% usage would represent a $ 1,500 balance. Increasing the credit limit from $ 5,000 to $ 10,000 would allow a $ 3,000 balance and still maintain 30% utilization. This is also the reason why you should not close your accounts, which will increase the percentage of total available credit that you are using - and which will reduce your score.

Negotiate a lower interest rate

However, the key to this strategy is getting more credit, but no longer using credit. In other words, if the limit goes up to $ 1,000, do not go out and half responsible for it. Think of the push as a way to save money when applying for a car loan, home loan or another form of long-term debt where a high credit score will probably lead to big savings through a rate of lower interest.

Chapter 10. How to Find Credit Cards with Guaranteed Approval?

What does true mean by promised approval? All credit cards come with some form of basic requirements before you are issued by a business. A key factor in those so-called secured credit cards is that the qualification requirements are usually minimal.

Most card issuers may demand that you have an active checking account to provide proof of income that meets a certain minimum amount. There is also the question how poor the reputation is, too. A credit score of between 300 (lowest FICO score) and 650 is generally considered poor credit. Some card issuers, however, will consider scores from 550 to 650 to be simply poor credit, and may consider you to be an unsecured credit card.

Fingerhut Credit Account

The Fingerhut Credit Card is specifically designed for those with bad credit. This credit card requires applicants to have a valid checking account and allows cardholders to use responsibly to build credit. Bad credit applicants can be accepted for initial credit lines of $300 or more and use wisely will raise that to more than $2,000 — without a security deposit being needed.

Milestone Mastercard – Less Than Perfect Credit Considered

The Milestone MasterCard provides a fast and easy application process and the use of all types of credit is encouraged. The card does not require a security deposit and is very welcoming to vulnerable creditors. The Milestone Card may be used anywhere Visa is approved, according to the credit available.

Total Visa Card

The Full Visa Card is another card that does not need a security deposit and provides all the perks of a Visa full-service card. The card allows borrowers to have a current checking account, and a one-time service fee is charged. The lines of credit available are based on your actual credit score and credit worthiness.

How to Properly Dispute Negative Account

If you find any errors in your credit report, you should contact the credit reporting agency and report the inaccuracy immediately.

Write a letter to the credit reporting agency that has your file and tell them which items you are disputing and why.

Be sure to provide the following identifying information:

- Your full name and address

- Your complete mailing addresses

- Your last address
- Your social security numbers
- Your date of birth
- The name of the creditor and account number of the disputed item
- Why you dispute the information
- Your signature

Check items that are potentially reporting incorrectly, outdated, unverifiable, misleading, merged, inaccurate or questionable. It is important to have a record of all your correspondence. Make sure you keep copies of your dispute letters and enclosures.

Send your dispute letters and other correspondence via certified mail, return receipt requested, so you can have a record of what the credit bureau received. And keep close track of the time that you sent the letter. The credit reporting agency must reinvestigate the items in question and inform you of the results of the investigation.

Request Method of Investigation

Sometimes the credit reporting agency will respond that they have verified the accuracy and completeness of the disputed item and that the information will remain in your file.

If the credit reporting agency sends you a letter that the item has been verified as accurate, according to FCRA you have the right to request their method of verification and they are obligated to reply to that request within 15 days.

The credit bureaus are required to provide the method of verification that includes the name, address, and telephone number of the data furnisher if requested by a consumer. Also, they must prove they received from the creditor a copy of an original dated contract with your signature on it.

As always, send the letter certified mail, return receipt requested, and keep a copy for your records.

Send A Notice of Intent to File A Complaint

If you are dissatisfied with the credit bureau's handling of your dispute, you can send them a Letter of Intent to File A Complaint with the Federal Trade Commission (FTC), the agency that regulates the credit bureaus. This fact alone might push them to delete the negative item.

If they still refuse to comply, you will need to file a complaint with the Federal Trade Commission. Visit the

FTC website to file your complaint against the credit bureau.

Contact an Attorney

If these methods failed to elicit a favorable response, write to the bureau informing them that you have consulted an attorney and found them to be willfully noncompliant with the FCRA. In many cases, this type of letter will cause the bureau to delete the item, as they believe you may pursue a lawsuit.

Your Rights When Dealing with Collection Agencies

Collection agencies often use aggressive methods to collect debts. They can harass you constantly and adversely impact your credit score. Do not let debt collectors intimidate you. Know your rights and stand up.

Chapter 11. What the Credit Bureaus and The Lawyers Do Not Want You to Know

The use of credit has become a cherished American way of life. Due to increased use of charge accounts – in the form of credit cards and other no-money-down inducements, it became necessary to issue reports concerning the credit history of consumers.

Credit reporting agencies were formed to supply these reports. Credit reporting agencies, often called credit bureaus, are agencies that collect information on credit users and sell it to retailers, banks, credit card companies, finance companies, and other lenders. The information is sold in the form of credit reports and it contains an evaluation mark of positive, negative, or neutral.

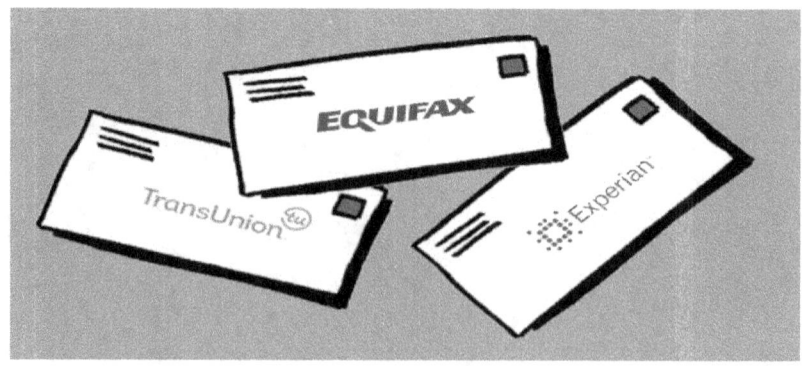

Credit bureaus freely exchange information with each other, about almost every adult in this country who has ever requested credit. They pass information to other bureaus when people move, for example. If you have a good credit record in your hometown, you can get credit anywhere in the United States.

Credit bureaus keep on file information supplied over time by your creditors, but they do not rate how good or bad a credit risk you are; they do not make any judgment on your ability to repay a loan. It is up to the potential creditor requesting the file, to decide whether to grant you credit. The three major national credit reporting agencies maintaining your credit records. All three work independently of each other in gathering information about you. They have vast databases that track the credit history of several hundred million people around the world.

Experian is the largest with $4.7 billion in revenues in 2013. **Equifax**, with $1.9 billion in revenue is the oldest of the three agencies and maintains information on over 400 million credit holders worldwide. **TransUnion** is the third largest credit bureau in the country with $1.1 billion in revenues.

What Creditors Look For

In order to establish a good credit reputation, you need a thorough understanding of the credit game. The theory most often used in determining your credit worthiness is sometimes referred to as the three C's of credit. These three C's are:

Character

Character is determined by the way you have handled your transactions in the past. Creditors will look at such things as how much you owe, how often you borrow, and how reliably you have repaid past debts. They also consider how long you have worked in your present job, residence at your present address, and whether you own or rent.

Capacity

This reflects your financial ability to repay your loan. Creditors will ask you to furnish information about your employment: Your occupation, the length of time you have held this or a last job, and how much you earn.

Capital

Capital refers to your assets which can serve as collateral for your loan. The credit grantor wants to know what valuable property or money other than your regular income could be used to secure your loan. Your assets include your house, jewelry, car, stocks and bonds, savings, and other valuables.

Credit grantors or lenders use different combinations of these facts in reaching their decisions. Each credit grantor extends credit based on their own polices and standards. One creditor may find you to be creditworthy, while another may deny you credit. If you do not have credit experience (character), you may still be granted credit on the basis of your capital and capacity until you establish a solid credit reputation.

Chapter 12. How Credit Scores Are Calculated

How is your credit score calculated? While it varies a little between the different credit reporting companies, the basic rules are the same. Some of the major factors that go into the algorithm to determine your score include things like debt level, credit history, and payment behavior. There is no consistent way in which they are measured since the weight of each is dependent on all the other credit factors available. Factors like ethnicity, religion and gender are not taken into consideration.

Your FICO score is a measure of the overall quality of your credit. While it is not the only available metric for determining credit score, it is the one that is most commonly used by a wide range of different lenders and companies when it comes to determining the level of risk that is associated with a given individual.

It is based on a handful of different categories at various levels of importance to the total. It has been determined that payment history is weighted with approximately 35 percent relevance, the amount owed has a 30 percent relevance, credit history length has a 15 percent relevance, abundance of new credit has a 10 percent relevance and the type of credit used has a 10 percent relevance.

It also factors in things such as delinquency, number of accounts you have in collections, bankruptcy and how long it has been since these problems appeared on your record. As such, the greater number of problems you have had in this regard, the worse your overall FICO score is going to be.

When it comes to the amount you currently owe to lenders, FICO takes into account the amount of debt you currently have as well as the types of accounts you hold and the number of different accounts that you currently hold.

To help you understand the scores better, here is a breakdown of the credit score ranges and what each means.

720 and Above Excellent

When you have this score, you get the best interest rates and repayment terms for all loans. This score can come in handy if you are hoping to make some major purchases. You will be able to get credit without any problems and at the lowest possible rates. But then, this score is extremely hard to establish. You will have to put in a lot of effort to maintain this score and still, you will not come anywhere close to 800. The most you can wish to come close to is 720 and remain there for as long as possible.

680-719-Good

When you are in this category, you will get good rates and terms but not as good as those with excellent scores. With this score, you can get favorable mortgage terms. You might not face as many problems but will have to be ready to run around from company to company to have your credit approved. Again, this score is not very common. You need to put in extra effort to get it over the 680 mark. If because of some erroneous charges you are not able to cross this limit, then you must try your best to get it cleared as soon as possible.

620-679-Average

When you are in this category, you can get fair mortgage terms and have it easy when buying smaller ticket items, (of course with no better rate than good and excellent scores). Take care not to slip down to the level where mortgage is unaffordable.

580-619-Poor

When you are at this level, you only get credit on the lenders' terms. You will probably pay more to access credit so be ready to pay more. Also, you should remember that you cannot access auto financing if your score goes lower than this range so you should work towards building it. This is where a large majority lie. Their score will be bad mostly owing to wrong entries. If you lie here, then you will have a tough time getting credit in your budget limits and will have to be ready to pay up a lot of money.

500-579-Bad

If your credit score is in this range, access to credit will cost you dearly. Actually, if you are looking for a 30-year mortgage, you could be looking at, at least 3% higher interest rates than how much you would pay if you had good credit. On the other hand, if you are looking for something short time like a 36-month auto loan, you will probably pay almost double the interest rate you would pay if you had good credit. So being here is probably the worst thing that can happen to your credit report. You cannot possibly be here and hope to get away with low interest rates.

Less than 500

If your credit score goes to this level, it is so bad that it might be almost impossible to get any type of financing. If you do, the interest rate will simply be unfathomable. You might have to spend 30 to 40 years trying to repay it. Your entire life will be dedicated toward repaying a loan and you might only get free by the time you are 50.

I am sure several of you are in this last range. But do not panic as help is at hand. You might wonder if it is possible for you to fix your score if you are in this category and the answer is yes! It is possible for you to improve your credit score and possibly enter the good range.

Chapter 13. Right Mindset for Credit Management

Financial problems can be and usually are overwhelming. To make these situations worse, most people do not even know where to begin to solve these financial dilemmas. Basic consumer debt will chain you into slavery and you could possibly spend your life held down by your own obligations to repay these loans.

The person or institution lending you the money is trusting that you have the ability to hold up your end of the bargain, basically.

Since your ability to repay a loan has been affected, either by the inability to pay or a series of misunderstandings other lenders will become skeptical when it comes to granting you a new credit.

What type of credit should you get? That depends on what you plan to do with the money. The most used types of credit are secured and signature credits. For smaller loans, there's no need for that, as no institution would like to end up with a store of household items, so they lend you money or issue a credit card in your name simply based on the strength of your credit so far.

You can take advantage of budgeting and other techniques, such as debt consolidation, debt settlement, credit counseling, and bankruptcy procedures. You just have to choose the best strategy that will work for you. When choosing from the various options, you have to consider your debt level, your discipline, and plans for the future.

Using consolidation or settlement strategies to pay down debts

Debt consolidation is another strategy that can be used to manage your debts. It involves combining two or more debts at a lower interest rate than you are currently at.

But it is worth doing your research and making some phone calls to see if there is a company that is willing to work with you. If you can lower your monthly bill to a manageable level, at an interest rate that is reasonable, that can make all the difference in handling your debt.

It is just that consolidation and settlement options rose in popularity during the recent financial crisis making it appear in more articles and news pieces than ever before.

Negotiate with Credit Companies

Another thing not a lot of people know is that you can negotiate with credit companies. So you are able to take the collection letter they send you or a past due notice that has been sent to you and discuss it with them. In many cases they will take a lower amount than what is on the bill just so that they can guarantee they will get something

If you talk to the collection agency and they agree to take a lesser amount you will have to send that payment in full. Make sure that when you send them the check you write out the words 'paid in full' on the check. Make a copy of the check for your own records as well. Once they cash that check your account is legally considered to be paid in full and they are no longer able to come after you for more money.

Cut the Credit Cards

Choose a card that will work anywhere such as a major credit card company.

The best thing to do is make one to two small purchases on your credit card every few months. Try to space out using different cards so that none of them get taken but you do not owe very much money each month.

Talking to Creditors

Tell them the reason why you are having a difficult time paying the debts. Most companies will negotiate a modified payment plan so monthly payments become more manageable. If you wait for the accounts to go into default, it can and most likely will affect your credit score negatively, which is what we are looking to avoid. Once in default, the collector will start calling.

Credit Counseling

Credit counseling is a service offered by some organizations to borrowers seeking advice on how they can manage their finances. It usually includes budgeting, workshops, and educational resources. A counselor must receive training and certification in budgeting, money and debt management, and consumer credit.

Debt Management Plan

The credit counselor negotiates with the creditors and drafts a payment schedule. Creditors may be amenable to waive some fees or reduce interest rates. Usually, a debt management plan takes about 4 years to be completed, depending on your amount of debt.

This is a great option for someone who would like to be "hands off" while repaying their debt and repairing their credit.

Debt Settlement Program

A debt settlement program can be risky, so you have to consider some factors before taking advantage of it. Many of these programs require that you deposit money on an account for at least 3 years before the debt settlement company can settle your debts.

Another aspect to consider is that some creditors will not negotiate for a debt settlement; therefore, the debt settlement company may not be able to pay some of your debts. In addition, some of these debt settlement companies pay off smaller debts first, leaving the large debts to continue growing.

The debt settlement company will suggest that you stop paying your creditors. This decision will result in a significant drop to your credit score. The debts will also incur fees and penalties for nonpayment. A debt settlement program is only as good as the debt settlement company that offers it.

Chapter 14. Delete Inquiries on Your Report

Hard Inquiries

Whenever a potential lender or a creditor asks to look into your credit report, it raises an inquiry with the credit bureau. The same will reflect in your report. There are two types of inquiries, either hard or soft inquiry.

If you apply for a line of credit, and the lender checks your credit report to decide if you are a potential candidate, is a hard inquiry. A hard inquiry will always show up on your credit report. A hard inquiry will affect your overall credit score. If you apply for a mortgage, credit card, auto loan, or any other form of credit, the lender will check your credit report and score. The lender does this with your permission. They will check your credit report with one or all of the major credit bureaus. Since this inquiry is related to a credit application, they are hard inquiries and will show up in your credit report. And since they show up on your credit report, it will influence your credit score.

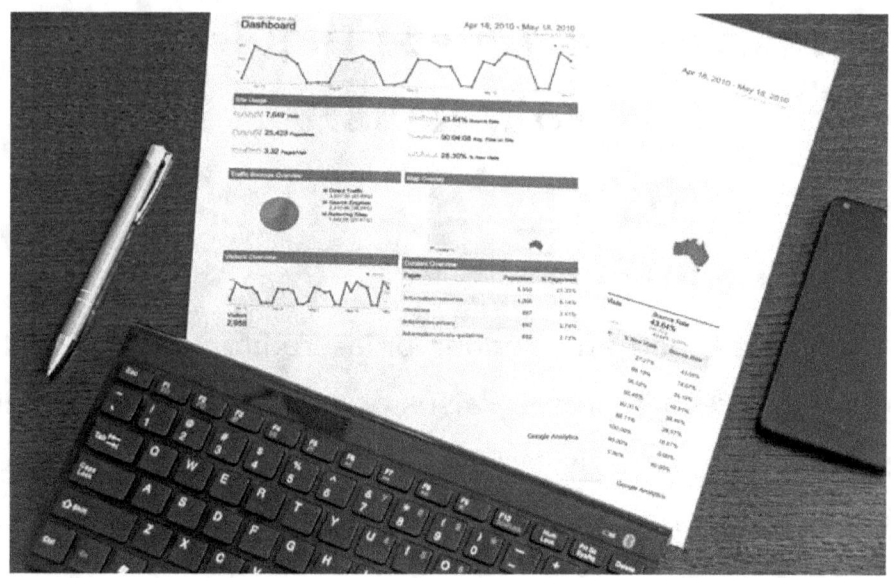

Now, let us look at the way hard inquiries affect your credit report. If there are too many hard inquiries about your credit report within a short period, then it is a red flag for potential lenders. Hard inquiries, especially multiple ones, can imply that you are looking to open multiple new accounts. If you start opening multiple accounts, it shows that you are in dire need of funds and that your financial position is not that good. It might also mean that you are overspending. So, it harms your credit report as well as your credit score.

You might be thinking that a person might make multiple inquiries about credit because he is shopping for the best deal on a loan. Credit rating models do consider this possibility. Most will accommodate multiple inquiries made within a short time frame for a line of credit involving a mortgage or a car loan. Numerous inquiries made about a specific credit product will be treated as a single inquiry and will have a relatively smaller effect on your credit report. Usually, you will not be denied credit because of the number of hard inquiries on your credit report. It is because a hard inquiry is only one of the many factors that are taken into consideration for generating your credit report as well as credit score.

Hard inquiries can stay on your credit report for around two years, but as time passes by, their effect also reduces. Even if you have several hard inquiries within a short period, this cannot be a reason for disqualifying you for credit by a lender. Your credit history, as well as the promptness of payments, are the other factors that are taken into consideration before you are either approved or rejected for a loan.

If the hard inquiry in the credit report is accurate, then you cannot have it removed. However, you can dispute a hard inquiry if it was started without your permission or if there was an error. If you notice a hard inquiry from an unfamiliar lender in your credit report, it is something you must look into immediately. It is often a sign of identity theft. So, if you find any inaccurate hard inquiries in your credit report, then you can raise a dispute about them. Upon investigation, if the bureau realizes that the hard inquiry was indeed inaccurate, then it will be removed from your report. When this happens, its effect will also be removed from your credit score.

Soft Inquiries

A soft inquiry occurs whenever you check your credit report. It also happens when you allow someone else to check your credit reports like a potential employer or a landlord. At times, different businesses, as well as financial institutions, have certain offers that they think will be helpful to you. In such cases, they will check your credit report for pre-approving you for any of those offers. This is also an example of a soft inquiry.

Since a soft inquiry does not directly relate to the application for a new line of credit, they are not usually visible on your credit report. However, there are certain exceptions to this rule. You are the only one who can view the soft inquiries. The two exceptions to this rule are as follows.

- An insurance company might be able to see the inquiries made about you by other similar companies.

- Any inquiry made by debt settlement agencies can be shared with your existing creditors. This can happen only with your prior authorization.

Since there never factored into the credit scoring models, they will not have any effect on your credit report. They are available for reference, but you cannot dispute soft inquiries except for the two mentioned above, soft inquiries cannot be viewed by anyone else.

Managing Inquiries

If you are worried that the hard inquiries are hurting your credit score, then you can take the following steps.

- Be prudent and apply for credit only when needed.

- If you are looking for a specific credit line like a mortgage or auto loan, then you do your rate shopping in a short period.

- Keep checking your credit report regularly to ensure that there are no inaccurate hard inquiries on it.

- Start managing the other important factors that influence your credit score.

If a hard inquiry took place without your approval, then you can remove it from your credit history. If you had no prior knowledge of the hard inquiry made about your credit report or your credit profile, then you have the right to have it removed. At times, you can also get these inquiries removed from the credit report that have been made because you were pressured into accepting an application process that you were not interested in. Here are all the instances of hard inquiries that you can remove from your credit report.

• Any inquiry that was made without your prior knowledge.

• Any inquiry that was made without your consent.

• Any inquiry that was made because you were pressured.

• The number of inquiries in your report exceeds the actual amount made.

If you notice an inaccurate hard inquiry on your credit report, then you can send a letter contacting the appropriate agency for its removal. When you are sending a message for removal, you can send it to the credit bureau as well as the lender. Here are the steps you must follow.

The first step is to send a letter for removal of the credit inquiry to the credit bureau and the lender through a certified mail service. A certified mail will record when the letter was sent as well as received. You can use this record as legal proof in case of any discrepancy. This comes in handy, especially when the receiver denies receiving the letter.

Before you send a notice for the removal of your credit inquiries, you need to notify the lender. You are obligated to notify the lender if you wish to take any legal action. Do not be surprised if the lender is not as responsive as the credit bureau. However, this is one step you must not ignore, and it is the right way to go about getting an inaccurate hard inquiry removed from your report.

While you are sending your letter for removal, please ensure that you attach a copy of your credit report with it. Highlight the discrepancy in the report or any other unauthorized inquiries. A credit bureau will have easy access to your account, but it helps investigators if you send a hard copy.

Please ensure that you are sending the letter to the right authority. If the discrepancy was in a report compiled by Equifax, then it does not make any sense to send a copy of the letter to TransUnion. Here are the addresses of the three major credit bureaus in the U.S.

The process of removal of any negative entry from your credit report is lengthy and time-consuming. So, if you like quick results, this process will be a lesson in patience. It might not seem like a couple of points will make much of a difference to your credit score, but they will soon add up to a significant number if left unchecked. Therefore, it is quintessential that you stay on top of any inquiries you make about the removal of negative entries on your credit report. If you want to improve your credit score and want to keep it high, then ensure that all the entries in your credit report are correct.

Notes: Making multiple hard inquiries within a short period is usually an indication of filing for bankruptcy. Numerous hard inquiries signify that you are running out of funds or have already run out of funds. It also shows that your financial position is highly unstable. If a person is looking for multiple means of credit at the same time for different reasons, it is an indication of bankruptcy. So, if you are making any hard inquiries within a short period, be mindful of this.

Chapter 15. Rebuild Your Credit

Credit card debts are probably seen as something that cause great distress. The good news is that you can break free from the bondage of debt. Apart from rebuilding your credit history, your mentality should be focused on getting out of debt and building wealth. Dumping debt is empowering. And you have the power to stay out of debt if you really want to.

The following are added information on how you can rebuild your credit and finally proclaim yourself, debt free.

Use Good Credit to Leverage Your Way Up

If you have gone through a bad experience about credit cards, you would probably associate the word "credit" with the word "bad". Good credit breeds good credit. Part of the technique is to use your credit and be wise enough to become a person of good standing. With a good credit rating, you are able to get the best interest rates on your loans and credit cards. Having good credit standing helps you become more aware of your status and keep to it. Collection calls are now a thing of the past. The constant feeling of worrying how to settle your monthly dues are no longer a major concern. Bills are paid off and you feel a certain kind of control, freedom, and peace of mind.

There Needs to Be an Activity and Constant Update

In order to rebuild your credit, do not let old information sit for a long time. Your credit report should always have recent activities listed for at least six months. Be active and generate good information. There has to be timely and consistent pattern of payments so you can be flagged for consistent payments. Having regular activity means your credit report gets fresh update on a monthly basis.

Get a Secured Credit Card

This is another way to prove that you are credit worthy. If getting a regular credit card is not possible, you may get a secured card. It works in a way that you deposit a certain amount in the bank, and in essence, allow you to borrow it back. Your credit limit depends on the money that you have deposited. Pay your monthly fees on time and request for a regular card after a year of no delay payments. Finally, the more important part is that you confirm with the credit union if they turn in your good standing information to the credit reporting agencies. Remember your purpose in getting the card – build your credit rating. So if they are not going to turn up on the credit report, this whole thing of rebuilding your credit is pointless.

Borrow a Small Installment Loan from Your Trusted Bank

This is another way towards a stellar credit report. It may seem odd at first but know that credit scores are calculated based on having different kinds of loans and not just credit cards. You can just opt to borrow a small amount from the bank and keep the length of the loan for at least a year. The goal is to establish a new credit path and have regular activity to spark your credit score.

Co-Sign a Loan with Someone

Just a word of caution: co-sign a loan with someone whom you know is responsible enough to take on debt and pay for it. Remember, when you co-sign, you share the debt. And, if they fail to repay the debt, the lending bank will come to you for full payment. Also, if your spouse or a family member is an authorized user of your credit card, you can make him/her a joint account holder. Getting credit under each person's name can give you good credit.

Completely Eliminate Your Debt for Life

If there is one method that would cure your debts and worries away that would have to be debt elimination. You can do this by allotting money meant for your bills. Or, if you have saved up for the rainy days, now is the time to take that out and lessen your debts. Paying them could save you with hundreds and thousands of dollars on interest rates. You would not want to pay high interest rates for life, don't you?

Apply the Debt Reduction Method

All you have to do is prepare a simple draft of your income statement showing your net worth, a balance sheet, and two letters from your CPA. Showing concrete statements is one of your most powerful tools in reducing your debt drastically. Just do not forget to consult your financial adviser about this.

Always Check for Identity Theft

There is a high probability that there could be an unexplained item (s) in your credit report that does not belong to you. Sad fact is that it is a bad credit score. If this happens, you could be denied credit and you are going to pay for it. So if there is something mysterious that you see in your credit report, call the credit card company immediately. You need to act fast because you could be a victim of identity theft. It is a real threat.

Avoid becoming a victim by following these safety tips:

- Do not disclose any personal information over the phone such as your social security number and credit card number.

- Almost all thefts occur online, so be smart when doing your online banking. Always log off your account once finished.

- Do not download anything that pops up on your computer.

- Change your password regularly.

- Run an antivirus or security software all the time.

- Do not use online banking when on a Wi-Fi network at public places.

Be Wiser When Handling Finances

You have probably learned your lesson the hard way. But what is important is that you learn from it and act on it. This way, you will not fall victim of this scrupulous scheme again and somehow learn how to play this tricky game.

Chapter 16. Protect Your Credit: Credit Monitoring

In addition to fraud alerts and credit freezes, you can invest in credit monitoring to protect your credit. It means monitoring and inspecting your credit history as shown on your credit report. In the end, that is really what it is all about, your credit report and more importantly unexpected changes to your credit report. A credit monitoring service provides this monitoring service for you (for a fee, of course). Most credit monitoring services report that they monitor and track your credit report daily.

What Happens with Credit Monitoring?

Once you sign up with a credit monitoring company, they pull all your information from all three credit reporting agencies and typically ask if you are in the process of applying for new credit. Often, they will ask you to check the credit report and verify the information. Of course, they will want to know about any activity you consider suspicious. Now, your new credit monitoring service has a baseline or starting point. Any changes to your credit report going forward could be flagged as possibly fraudulent. Depending on the options available and the monitoring plan you chose, you will be alerted to any suspicious activity that could affect your credit report.

The credit monitoring companies typically are on the alert for:

- New credit inquiries

- Delinquencies

- Negative information that suddenly shows up

- Employment changes

- New credit accounts

- Increased credit lines at existing accounts

- Other changes to your credit report that could be considered a red flag for identity theft

You should note that one reason credit monitoring services have become so popular lately is their alerts for suspicious activity on your credit report is viewed as a counter to identity theft. Some credit monitoring companies even promote their services with this claim.

Advantages

- Constant Tracking - All of your credit reports are constantly tracked. Depending on your choice of credit monitoring companies and plans, this monitoring could be daily or weekly.

- Increased Knowledge - about your own credit. During the time you use a credit monitoring service, you will gain an incredibly valuable firsthand knowledge of how personal credit actually works. Simply by watching the reports provided from your credit monitoring service, you will see in real time how your credit report changes. You will see how even small actions on your part can have a sizeable effect on your credit score. For example, you can watch your credit score drop right after you applied for four different department store credit cards.

- It Does not Cost, it Saves - Yes, this is a tired old cliché, yet here it truly works. Consider it this way: suppose you use your new knowledge of how your personal credit works, how small things affect your credit score, and that sort of thing to get a better loan rate. Really, it is that easy. For example, let us say you use your newfound credit wisdom to raise your credit score by 75 points. Then, you refinance your home and get a lower interest rate that saves you hundreds of dollars a month or thousands of dollars over the term of your mortgage.

- Identity Theft Protection - Since your credit report is under constant scrutiny, detection of possible fraudulent activity happens much faster. The credit monitoring service helps you both detect and minimize damage from malicious use of your personal financial information. Additionally, many credit monitoring companies offer legal protections and financial reimbursements. These reimbursements can range from $25,000 to $1,000,000. Surely you have seen the advertisements with the big-name credit monitoring service offering their one-million-dollar guarantee.

- Faster Resolution of Errors - Should you spot an error on one of your many reports sent to you by your credit monitoring service, most of them will assist you in correcting the error.

- No More Guesswork - Since you are paying for professional credit monitoring, you do not have to guess what is going on with your credit score or your credit report. Additionally, since your credit monitoring service will alert you for any suspicious activities, you are always aware of what is happening with your credit.

- Less Hassle for You - Yes, credit monitoring can be done yourself as will be explained shortly. However, paying for a credit monitoring service eliminates one more thing for you to do.

Disadvantages

- Price - Of course, all of the services provided by credit monitoring companies comes at a price. Price is one common complaint against credit monitoring companies. Each company sets their own pricing structure. Also, many of them offer different levels of service at different price points.

- Information Disparity - The information available from one credit monitoring service can be vastly different from another credit monitoring service. Make sure you know what you are paying for when you sign up for a credit monitoring plan.

- Cancellation Issues - There are various reports (complaints) from past customers of some credit monitoring services regarding the difficulty encountered in cancelling the service.

- Micromanagement Time Wastes - Because your new credit monitoring service provides you with frequent reports and analysis, you may end up trying to micromanage your credit score. This micromanagement could end up costing you a lot of time with few if any substantive changes to your credit score.

- False Sense of Security - Since you are paying for a credit monitoring service, the tendency is to fall into the trap of that is all you need to do to protect yourself. Identity theft protection involves additional areas beyond your credit report that you still need to monitor.

- A Credit Monitoring Service Cannot Do it as Fast as You Might Want - It is not yet possible to monitor a person's credit history on a real time basis. For one thing, many creditors only report information on existing clients weekly or even monthly.

- A Credit Monitoring Service is not the Final Solution - Even the very best credit monitoring service is not capable of fully identifying all fraudulent activity. Consider that there are many credit details that are never even reported to a credit reporting agency.

Conclusion

In the times we live in, it is almost impossible to live without having at least one credit. The unstable rates of unemployment can affect everyone, which is why more and more Americans are confronted with the problem of bad credit. The unfortunate fact is that more and more people choose to do nothing about it and live with bad credit for a long time. What you have to understand is that bad credit gets even worse over time as its grave consequences will be felt more and more, leading to things such as the impossibility to get a new credit, refinance an old credit, rent an apartment or get a job. This is why you should act in a time and take care of your finances, especially in the context of a shaky national and international economy.

Fixing your credit is the best solution and should become more popular in the United States, because I think it can really make a difference for a great number of people. Credit repair might seem complicated to some and it definitely takes time to finalize, but nothing great is ever accomplished without a little bit of work. Also, there is no specialist that can claim that a credit repair done in one way or another has a one hundred percent success rate. If they do, be careful with people trying to scam you for money while claiming they are repairing your bad credit.

The benefits of fixing your credit might reveal themselves over an extended period of time but by carefully doing all the steps describes in here will eventually clear your credit and increase your chances of you ending up with increased scores on a credit application. It will also help you with finding a job, even though your credit is not entirely repaired. When someone is evaluating your credit report and sees the written statements and all the work you have put in for the process, it shows how responsible and preoccupied you are about your finances and says a lot about who you are.

Remember to be consistent and make sure to rid yourself of all the unnecessary expenses that you have. Try to establish a new and fresh way to keep track of your payments. Do not be afraid to act, for it is only then that you will be able to see the result. Always think positive, and do not let failure hold you back from your goal to be credit worthy once again. In the end, all the efforts are truly worth it. Not only will you have peace of mind and feel better about your life, but the more important goal is to have a trouble-free process in acquiring a new house or car because of your good and trustworthy credit. What is more, because of that good credit standing, you might even land the job or start the business that you have been dreaming of. Isn't that something to look forward to?

Many people become enthusiastic about credit repairing and when they see the effort involved and the time required on the journey to good credit, they get discouraged and give up. Others give up after the first negative response from a creditor or credit report agency and some even go through with it but stop doing things to improve their credit when they've finished the process and still haven't managed to fix all the negative items. The important thing about the whole process is to stay motivated and continue improving.

Make sure that you are paying attention to your credit. It is going to be extremely important throughout your life so that you can have fun and do the things you enjoy.

www.ingramcontent.com/pod-product-compliance
Lightning Source LLC
Chambersburg PA
CBHW071417210526
45465CB00001B/423